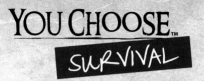

YOU CHOOSE™
SURVIVAL

☞ W9-BRX-094

Can You Survive

STORM CHASING?

An Interactive Survival Adventure

by Elizabeth Raum

Consultant:
Martin A. Baxter, PhD
Assistant Professor of Meteorology
Department of Earth and Atmospheric Science
Central Michigan University

CAPSTONE PRESS
a capstone imprint

You Choose Books are published by Capstone Press,
151 Good Counsel Drive, P.O. Box 669, Mankato, Minnesota 56002.
www.capstonepub.com

Copyright © 2012 by Capstone Press, a Capstone imprint.
All rights reserved. No part of this publication may be reproduced in whole or in part,
or stored in a retrieval system, or transmitted in any form or by any means, electronic,
mechanical, photocopying, recording, or otherwise, without written permission of the
publisher. For information regarding permission, write to Capstone Press, 151 Good
Counsel Drive, P.O. Box 669, Dept. R, Mankato, Minnesota 56002.

Books published by Capstone Press are manufactured with paper
containing at least 10 percent post-consumer waste.

Library of Congress Cataloging-in-Publication Data
Raum, Elizabeth.
  Can you survive storm chasing? : an interactive survival adventure /
by Elizabeth Raum.
      p. cm. — (You choose : survival)
  Includes bibliographical references and index.
  ISBN 978-1-4296-6587-2 (library binding)
  ISBN 978-1-4296-7347-1 (paperback)
  1. Emergency management—Juvenile literature. 2. Storms—Juvenile
literature. I. Title.
  HV551.2.R38 2012
  613.6'9—dc22   2011010182

Summary: Describes the fight for survival when caught in tornadoes, hurricanes, and
flash floods.

Editorial Credits
Brenda Haugen, editor; Veronica Correia and Bobbie Nuytten, designers; Wanda
Winch, media researcher; Laura Manthe, production specialist

Photo Credits
Alamy: Adrian Sherratt, 95; AP Images: Imaginechina, 79, Jeff Gentner, 74, Lori
Mehmen, 23; Capstone Studio: Karon Dubke, 103, 105; Corbis: Dallas Morning News/
Danny Gawlowski, 17, Jim McDonald, 55, Jim Reed Photography/Jim Reed, cover;
Digital Vision (Getty Images), 6; Getty Images Inc: Joe Raedle, 48, MCT/Forth
Worth Star-Telegram/Ron Jenkins, 83, National Geographic/Carsten Peter, 33, The
Washington Post/Jahi Chikwendiu, 87; iStockphoto: Steve Shepard, 91; Photolibrary:
Oxford Scientific (OSF)/Warren Faidley, 72, SuperStock Inc/Christopher Harris, 42;
Shutterstock: forestpath, 52, Neo Edmund, 61, pashabo, page design element, Tad
Denson, 67, Yury Zap, 100; Steve Molenaar, 12

Printed in the United States of America in Stevens Point, Wisconsin.
032011   006111WZF11

TABLE OF CONTENTS

About Your Adventure 5

Chapter 1
Amazed by Weather 7

Chapter 2
Tornado! 13

Chapter 3
Hurricane! 43

Chapter 4
Flood! 75

Chapter 5
Survival Guide 101

Real Survivors 106
Survival Quiz 108
Read More 109
Internet Sites 109
Glossary...110
Bibliography..111
Index..112

About Your
ADVENTURE

YOU are a meteorology student who is fascinated by storms. To learn more about weather events, you need to experience them firsthand. But will you be able to survive the dangerous situations?

In this book you'll deal with extreme survival situations. You'll explore how the knowledge you have and the choices you make can mean the difference between life and death.

Chapter One sets the scene. Then you choose which path to read. Follow the directions at the bottom of each page. The choices you make will change your outcome. After you finish one path, go back and read the others for new experiences and more adventures.

YOU CHOOSE the path you
take through your adventure.

Dark clouds can suddenly unleash powerful storms.

CHAPTER 1

Amazed by Weather

As soon as you hear a clap of thunder, you're out the door watching the sky. You've always been amazed by the weather. Your Uncle Dave is a meteorologist. When you were in grade school, he showed you how to keep accurate weather records.

In high school you read books about the weather, watched the Weather Channel on TV, and listened to weather reports on the radio. When it was time for college, you chose Central Michigan University's meteorology program. You have one more year of college. Then you'll be a meteorologist just like your uncle.

Turn the page.

You've seen some powerful storms. When you were 10, a tornado struck your grandparents' home. "It destroyed the dining room wall," Grandpa said, "but it never even touched the dishes on the table."

Tornadoes are the most violent storms on Earth. They often develop from supercell thunderstorms. Supercells can occur when warm, moist air rises to meet cold, dry air. About 15 percent of supercells produce tornadoes. The United States has about 1,000 tornadoes a year. Most occur along Tornado Alley, which runs north from Texas. But tornadoes can strike anywhere. As a meteorologist you will give advance warnings so people can seek shelter before a storm hits.

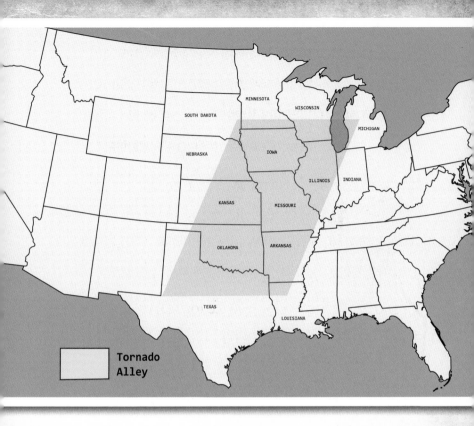

Tornado Alley

You've also experienced a flash flood. The power of the fast-moving water surprised you. It tore a garage off its foundation and carried it 2 miles downstream. Flash floods kill about 200 Americans a year, and they can happen anywhere.

Turn the page.

One storm you've never seen is a hurricane. Hurricanes are the biggest storms on Earth. Some are more than 500 miles wide. Many of these tropical storms form over warm ocean waters off the coast of Africa. These are the hurricanes that sometimes strike the United States. As the moisture rises, more air moves in to take its place. This creates a strong wind. As the wind circles, it draws more and more moisture from the water's surface. If the storm remains over warm water, it becomes larger and more powerful. But when the storm crosses cold water or land, it loses power and gradually fades away.

Like tornadoes, hurricane winds do lots of damage, but the storm surge may be even more dangerous. A storm surge is a type of flood. It occurs when ocean water is blown inland. Some areas near the Atlantic Ocean and the Gulf of Mexico are less than 10 feet above sea level. The surge can cause severe flooding in low-lying areas.

You'll have opportunities to learn about all three types of storms firsthand. You can't wait to spend your life predicting storms—but first, you'll need to survive the summer.

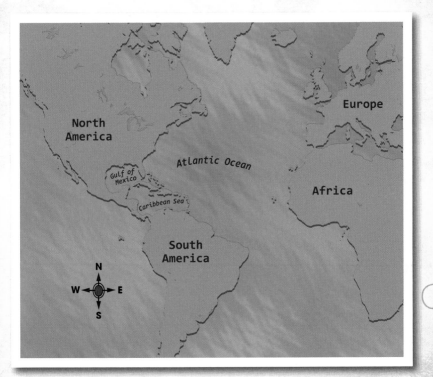

*To experience a tornado, turn to page **13**.*

*To encounter a hurricane, turn to page **43**.*

*To face a flash flood, turn to page **75**.*

A tornado touches down in rural Minnesota.

CHAPTER 2

Tornado!

You spot a flyer on the college bulletin board:

SUMMER JOB OPENING

Wanted: van driver for Wild Tornado Tours

Call: Steve Drake, Owner and Tour Leader

When you call the number, Steve explains that his company brings tourists close to the action. "Tornado tourists want pictures. They want to experience the fright and thrill of being close to a monster twister. Each tour lasts 10 days, and we try to satisfy our customers."

Turn the page.

The job sounds perfect. You'll be seeing tornadoes up close and earning money at the same time. The Wild Tornado Tours van contains mobile Internet access, laptop computers, storm-tracking software, and a GPS mapping system. Steve knows how to find twisters using this equipment. "We find them and get as close as we can," he says. "But safety is important too. With this equipment we can track the storms and avoid getting hurt." That sounds good to you.

In mid-May, you drive to Kansas City, Missouri, where you meet the first group of tornado tourists. Tomi is from Japan, Phil is from New York, and Pamela is from California.

"We'll zigzag across the Midwest, going where the storms lead us," Steve says. "We'll cover lots of miles fast. We have to if we want to see tornadoes."

On the first day, Steve directs you to take I-35 north. "There are storms forming in Minnesota. Tomorrow may be our lucky day!"

You reach Minnesota by nightfall and spend the night in a motel. Clear blue skies greet you in the morning. "Was the prediction wrong?" Pamela asks.

Steve shakes his head. "Don't let the sunshine fool you. Tornadoes often occur on days that start out sunny. The sun heats the ground, which adds strength to afternoon thunderstorms. But every tornado is different. Sometimes huge hailstones fall just before the tornado strikes. In other cases, there's hail, but no tornado. Sometimes strong winds come before the twister. Other times the air is so still that it's creepy."

15

Turn the page.

"But they all have a funnel," Tomi says.

"Yes. But every funnel is unique," Steve replies. "Some look like the one in the movie *The Wizard of Oz*. Others look like ropes hanging beneath a cloud. Sometimes two or three snakelike tornadoes twist and twirl together. They look kind of like a braid."

Steve checks several tornado-chasing Web sites on his computer. Then he connects to the National Weather Service Web site. "The National Weather Service is reporting a supercell forming near Northfield," he tells you.

You speed toward Northfield. The tourists prepare their cameras while Steve checks the radar. "It's a big one," he says. The sky grows darker.

"Pull over," Steve says. "We'll watch from here."

Storm chasers use the latest equipment to track storms.

Everyone piles out of the van and sets up their cameras at the edge of the road. You spot a wall cloud—a low-hanging cloud that develops just before a tornado forms.

Turn the page.

The wall cloud is large, dark, and rotating. You see the flickering greenish light of lightning inside of it. A tornado often strikes within 10 to 20 minutes after the wall cloud appears. Suddenly a funnel drops out of the cloud. It twists like a snake. Another dips down beside it. "Tornadoes!" you shout. "Coming this way!"

Steve, Tomi, and Pamela dash for the van. Phil hesitates. "One more picture," he begs.

To let him take another photo, go to page 19.

To insist on leaving, turn to page 21.

"OK, 30 seconds," you say, keeping your eye on the funnel. It's getting closer by the second. Finally Phil packs up and rushes with you back to the van. You take off before he shuts the door.

"It's coming straight at us!" Pamela screams.

You push the accelerator to the floor. The tornado is huge. It could pick up your van and toss it into the air. Your heart is pounding so loudly that you can't hear anything else.

You race down the road, trying to put distance between the van and the funnel. The average tornado speed is about 30 miles per hour, but they can travel much faster. Your speedometer reads 70 miles per hour. At last the funnel veers to the east. Everyone cheers. It was a close call—too close. You won't try to outrun a tornado again.

Turn the page.

On the fifth day of the 10-day tour, you're driving through Iowa when the sky darkens. Huge clouds form overhead. You see flickering around the clouds' edges. Then rain starts pouring down. Your windshield wipers are slapping against the window, but you can barely see the road. You slow down.

"What are you doing?" Steve asks. "Don't slow down. Keep going."

"But we won't be able to see a tornado in heavy rain like this," you say.

"Of course we'll see it," Steve says. "Drive on."

*To drive on, turn to page **28**.*

*To pull into a restaurant, turn to page **29**.*

Steve is the boss, but he's more willing to take chances than you are. Besides, you're driving, and safety is your first concern. "We leave now!" you shout. The tourists snap pictures through the van windows as you speed away.

"Good call," Steve says when you stop for lunch. Over sandwiches, Steve decides to drive southwest.

By noon the next day, you're driving across Nebraska toward western Kansas. "From there we'll go to Oklahoma, and if we still haven't found a tornado, we'll go to Texas," Steve says. You know Oklahoma and Texas average more tornadoes than most other states. You check the radar screen. There's a line of supercell thunderstorms over western Kansas. The National Weather Service has issued a tornado watch. This means that weather conditions are likely to produce a tornado.

By the time you reach Interstate 70 near Hays, Kansas, the watch has become a warning. That means that a tornado has been sighted or can be seen on radar. "Look for a funnel," Steve says.

"There!" you yell. The funnel is shaped like an elephant's trunk. It dangles out of a huge black cloud to the west and reaches clear to the ground. At first the funnel looks skinny, but it seems to grow wider as it moves closer. It looks less like an elephant's trunk and more like a giant ice cream cone.

You pull over. Everyone piles out to take pictures. But when the tornado veers northeast, Steve orders everyone back inside the van. "Let's follow it!" he says.

The tornado travels parallel to the van. "We have to get out of here," you tell Steve. You know that most tornado deaths occur in cars or mobile homes.

The size of tornadoes varies greatly.

"We're fine," Steve says. "This is what they're paying to see!"

In the back seat, the tourists click their cameras. The winds roar. Someone yells, "Look! It just hit that barn!" Boards and other debris fly through the air. The funnel veers toward you.

Turn the page.

"There's an underpass ahead!" Pamela yells. "We can wait beneath it until the storm passes!"

"No!" you shout back. "An underpass is one of the worst places to be. The bridge above could collapse. Even if it doesn't, wind speeds increase in the openings beneath bridges. It's a death trap."

"Pull over now!" Steve shouts. "There's a parking lot just ahead."

You see the parking lot for Wilson's Lumber. But you also see a road off to the right. You might escape by driving at a right angle to the tornado's direction of movement.

To veer to the right, go to page **25**.

To go into the parking lot, turn to page **30**.

You yank the steering wheel to the right and swerve onto the other road. Wind batters the van, but you keep control. You speed ahead. When you glance in the rearview mirror, all you see is swirling debris. It was too close a call, and it only worked because the roads weren't crowded. It's never smart to try to outrun a tornado. You were lucky.

Steve checks his equipment. "Let's find another one," he says. Radio announcers all over the area are broadcasting tornado warnings. Several tornadoes have touched down.

The rain has turned to a drizzle. "Funnel to the east! It's a whopper!" you shout.

Turn the page.

The funnel is biggest at the top where it connects to the cloud. It gets gradually smaller until it reaches the ground. Dust and dirt swirl at the base as the tornado churns the earth and everything in its path. "It's heading straight for Hays!" Steve says.

You pull over so that the tourists can take photos. The power of nature amazes you. But it also scares you. This tornado is a killer. The tourists pile back into the van when the funnel moves on. You begin driving south. "Get off at the next exit," Steve says. "We need gas."

Once you leave the Interstate, tree branches litter the road. You see a downed electric pole. Its wires drag along the ground. Accidentally touching or even getting too close to live wires can kill you. "This just happened," Steve says as he calls 911.

A little girl waves you over from the side of the road. "Help me!" she pleads. "The tornado blew our house down. My mom is trapped underneath." She points to a pile of rubble nearby.

It's getting dark. Glass and twisted metal make the debris dangerous. You reach for the flashlight that's in the emergency kit. Where is it?

You hear the woman moan. Her cries are weak. "Please hurry!" the girl says.

To begin moving debris, turn to page 32.

To keep searching for a flashlight, turn to page 40.

"Let's go!" everyone yells. Maybe you're being too cautious. You step hard on the gas pedal. The van leaps forward. Golf ball-sized hailstones pound on the roof. Hail sometimes comes just before a tornado hits. You should have stopped sooner.

"Funnel ahead!" Pamela shouts. It was hiding in the rain, and now it's coming right at you.

"Back up!" Steve yells.

You slam the van into reverse and stomp on the gas pedal.

"Faster!" Steve shouts.

You're not going to make it. There's a parking lot behind you.

To pull into the parking lot, turn to page **30.**

To keep going, turn to page **31.**

You pull into a small restaurant's parking lot. Maybe the rain will let up by the time you finish lunch. The waitress is about to take your order when hail smashes into the restaurant's roof. Hail is a sign that you may be near the storm's main updraft. It's time to get to safety. "I'm going to pick up some hailstones!" Tomi exclaims as he runs outside.

To go after him, turn to page 33.

To seek safety, turn to page 34.

You pull into the parking lot in front of Wilson's Lumber. It's a large warehouse with metal walls and a wide tin roof. The building probably doesn't have a basement or safe room. Is the roof strong enough to protect you from a tornado? Your other option is a farm field across from the parking lot.

You have just seconds to decide. There's no time to ask the others.

To go inside Wilson's Lumber, turn to page **35**.

To run into the farm field, turn to page **36**.

You have to get away from the tornado. You keep the van in reverse. If you can back up fast enough, you may escape.

As you try desperately to steer, the wind lifts the front end of the van into the air. Then it tilts the van toward the passenger side and slams it into a ditch. The last thing you hear before you black out is Pamela's scream.

When you regain consciousness a few minutes later, you're still belted into the driver's seat. It takes rescuers an hour to free you from the car. At the hospital you learn that Steve, Phil, and Tomi were killed in the crash. Pamela is in critical condition. Your leg is crushed. You'll probably never walk without a cane. You should have followed your instincts and not tried to outrun the tornado.

THE END

To follow another path, turn to page 11.
To read the conclusion, turn to page 101.

The little girl is frantic. You begin pulling boards aside to reach the woman. You can't see anything. It's getting darker by the minute.

"This will help!" Phil says, pulling a lighter from his pocket.

"No! There might be a gas leak!"

But it's too late. A spark from the lighter ignites gas leaking from a damaged fuel tank. The fireball kills you, the woman, and Phil. Using a flashlight could have saved you.

THE END

To follow another path, turn to page 11.
To read the conclusion, turn to page 101.

You rush outside after Tomi. "Come back!" you shout. "We have to get to safety." You reach out to grab him, but his shirt slips through your fingers. Your ears begin popping. Then you hear a sound like a freight train's roar. The tornado is here!

A tornado's wind speed can be more than 200 miles per hour.

Turn to page **37**.

It's not safe to go outside. You run to the door and call to Tomi. He turns back. "Then I'll watch from here," he says, standing in front of the restaurant's big picture windows.

"If the tornado strikes, this glass will shatter," you explain impatiently.

"But I came all the way from Japan to see tornadoes," he says. "Once I see a funnel, I'll run for cover."

You know it's not safe to stay, but perhaps you can convince him to move in time to avoid injury.

To stay with Tomi, turn to page **37**.

To run to the basement, turn to page **38**.

You're already at the lumber store's door when you realize that you are alone. The tourists have followed Steve into an open field. It's too late to turn around now. You step inside the building. There aren't any people around. You crouch beneath a counter. The metal walls shriek as the funnel tears them away. The roof crashes in. Lumber tumbles off the shelves and lands on the counter, crushing you beneath it. You are the only one of your group not to survive the storm.

THE END

To follow another path, turn to page 11.
To read the conclusion, turn to page 101.

A warehouse, gym, cafeteria, or any other building with a wide-span roof is dangerous during a tornado. The roof is likely to collapse in high winds. You choose the field. Your ears begin to pop, and a loud roar fills the air. It's important to stay near the ground. You lie flat and cover your head. The wind tugs at you, ripping the shirt off your back. The funnel drags you several feet before letting go. After it passes, you stand up and survey the damage. To your relief, everyone survived. You made the right choice.

THE END

To follow another path, turn to page 11.
To read the conclusion, turn to page 101.

The view of the approaching storm is fantastic. "There's the funnel!" someone cries. It twists and curls, swerves to the left, and then turns right.

"Run!" you yell. In the confusion, you trip over a chair and fall. Pain shoots through your ankle. You crawl beneath a table as the winds pull nails out of the building's siding. The walls shake. You're lifted into the air as the building disappears around you.

Turn to page 39.

You follow the restaurant staff to the basement. A basement is a good place to wait out a tornado. If there's no basement, a bathroom offers some protection. The walls have extra framing, and the plumbing holds everything together.

You choose a spot well away from the windows. Then you cover your head with your arms and tuck your body into a small ball. Someone tosses a blanket over you. You hear windows shatter and nails screech as the winds pull them out of the wood. Are people screaming or is that the wind? There's a huge crash above. Seconds later, the wind stops. "Help me!" a woman cries. "I'm trapped!" You rush up the stairs. The restaurant is a mess, and it's pitch dark. The woman must be trapped beneath the rubble.

Turn to page **40.**

The howling winds pick you up and slam you to the ground. Seconds later bricks rain down on you. You don't feel them. You're already unconscious.

The next day rescue workers uncover your body beneath a pile of debris. The National Weather Service rated the tornado an EF5, which is the strongest tornado. An EF5 has winds of more than 200 miles per hour. It can lift houses off their foundations and throw cars more than 100 yards. You were not the only person to die when the EF5 hit town.

THE END

To follow another path, turn to page 11.
To read the conclusion, turn to page 101.

If you reach into the debris without a light, you might touch a live wire or cut yourself on glass or twisted metal. It's better to take an extra minute to find a flashlight. When you do, you begin removing debris. It takes you about 10 minutes to free the woman. By that time paramedics have arrived to take her to the hospital. She'll live. It was a close call, but everyone in your group survived the twister too.

When you return home, you join Skywarn, an organization for individuals trained to spot tornadoes and other severe weather. Whenever you see signs that a tornado may be approaching, you call the National Weather Service on your cell phone. You know from experience that advance warnings save lives.

WHAT TO DO IF YOU
Hear a Tornado Warning or See a Tornado Funnel

IN A HOME WITH A BASEMENT
Go to the basement. Cover yourself with a mattress or blankets. Stay away from windows.

IN A HOME WITHOUT A BASEMENT
Move to a small room or hallway on the lowest floor. Get under a sturdy piece of furniture and cover yourself with a mattress or blankets. Stay away from windows. If you have a bathtub, get in it and pull a mattress over it.

IF YOU ARE OUTSIDE OR IN A CAR
Lie flat in a nearby ditch or depression. Get as far away from buildings and trees as possible. Cover your head with your arms.

IF YOU ARE IN A MOBILE HOME OR LARGE WAREHOUSE-TYPE BUILDING
Leave immediately. Go to a nearby shelter if possible. If not, lie on the ground as far from buildings and trees as possible. Cover your head.

THE END

To follow another path, turn to page 11.
To read the conclusion, turn to page 101.

Hurricanes can drop more than 2 trillion gallons of rain a day.

CHAPTER 3

Hurricane!

Uncle Dave is the chief meteorologist at a TV station on Florida's Gulf Coast. "The station manager has enough money in the budget to hire an intern. Do you want the job?" he asks. You are grateful for the opportunity and say yes.

As soon as you arrive in Florida, training begins. Dave teaches you the basics of TV weather reporting. It doesn't take long before you begin doing live reports from the harbor, the golf course, and the beach. So far it's been all sunshine and blue skies.

In mid-August a tropical storm develops in the northwestern Caribbean Sea. You follow the storm on radar. "This could be a major hurricane," Dave says. Hurricanes can happen at any time, but the main season begins on June 1 and runs through November 30. On August 18 the National Hurricane Center declares the storm a hurricane. They name it Fred.

"What category is the hurricane?" you ask Dave. He says it's a Category 3. The Saffir-Simpson Hurricane Wind Scale is based on wind speeds. The scale divides hurricanes into five categories. Category 5 is the worst. Category 3 storms have winds of 111 to 130 miles per hour. These wind speeds are likely to cause injury and death to people, livestock, and pets.

"How long before it hits?" you ask.

"It's traveling at 10 miles per hour," Dave replies. "The National Hurricane Center places us within the Track Forecast Cone. That means that the hurricane is headed our way, but they can't say exactly when or where it will strike. But this one looks like it may be here in less than 20 hours."

Saffir-Simpson Scale

Category	Winds	Summary
1	74-95 mph	Very dangerous winds will produce some damage
2	96-110 mph	Extremely dangerous winds will cause extensive damage
3	111-130 mph	Devastating damage will occur
4	131-155 mph	Catastrophic damage will occur
5	>155 mph	Catastrophic damage will occur

Turn the page.

City officials order a mandatory evacuation. People living within 1 mile of the coast are required to leave. "That's thousands of people," Dave says. "But I doubt everyone will leave. Many people think they'll be safe, so they stay. This station is 4 miles from the coast, so we should be safe from flooding. I'll be giving warnings all day and all night. I hope people will pay attention."

The news director sends a team of reporters to interview people at Sunset Beach. He sends another team to talk to homeowners in the Scenic Bay neighborhood, within a mile of the bay.

"Be careful," Dave warns you. "Don't take any chances."

*To go to the beach, go to page **47**.*

*To interview homeowners, turn to page **51**.*

You and Josh, the camera operator, drive to the beach. Strong waves are rolling in, but the sky is still blue. Sunbathers sprawl across the sand. Josh sets up the camera and scans the beach while you describe the scene to television viewers. "It seems like just another day at the beach," you say.

But in an hour or two the wind picks up. Your on-air report shows beach umbrellas whipping in the wind and people preparing to go home. Two small children run through the waves while their father watches from shore. "Aren't you concerned about the hurricane?" you ask.

"No," he says. "The kids are having a great time. I'm not going to drag them away from their vacation."

A hurricane's winds can reach more than 155 miles per hour.

"It's going to get worse," you say, but he waves you away. Surfers also seem unwilling to leave. "Best waves all summer," one says. Another adds, "We should have a hurricane every day."

You call your uncle. "People aren't taking the warnings seriously," you tell him.

"We're getting the same reports from all over the city. If Fred makes a direct hit, thousands could die in the storm surge as high winds push seawater a mile or more inland. Floodwaters could reach a depth of more than 20 feet."

You continue to do live reports all afternoon. Rain starts falling around 5:00 p.m. The rain clears the beaches better than the warnings. By 6:00 winds are whipping your shirt, and the rain is blowing sideways. Josh swivels the camera to show boat owners frantically tying their boats to the dock.

"Better call it a day," Uncle Dave says when you check in. "The National Hurricane Center upgraded Fred to a Category 4. It's not safe on the beach." It is exciting, though. You're tempted to stay and watch the storm for a while longer.

Josh puts the camera away. "We have to cross the bay. Traffic on the bridge will be heavy. The sooner we leave, the better," he says.

To stay on the beach, turn to page **54**.

To return to the station, turn to page **62**.

Officials have ordered thousands of people to pack up and leave. Most live within a mile of the water. Are people leaving? It's your job to find out. Josh, the cameraman, grew up in Scenic Bay. He suggests that you go to Shore Drive. The houses face the bay. A storm surge is likely to send seawater rushing into the bay, flooding the neighborhood.

You park and walk along the seawall. Waves pound against the concrete barriers and splash onto the sidewalk. The wind is so strong that Josh has trouble setting up the camera for shots of the bay. A man across the street nails plywood over his windows while his children play in the yard. A woman packs her car.

"Of course we're leaving," she says. "If Hurricane Fred strikes, this whole neighborhood will be underwater."

Turn the page.

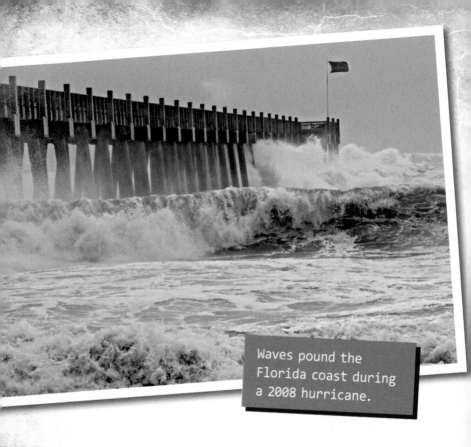

Waves pound the Florida coast during a 2008 hurricane.

Her neighbor, an elderly man, sits on his porch. "I'm not leaving," he says. "I have enough emergency supplies to last me a week." About half the people are leaving. Others say they may leave later. If they wait too long, the roads will be flooded.

The afternoon passes quickly as you give live reports from Scenic Bay. The storm is still on track for a direct hit. Water splashes over the seawall onto the streets. Then it starts to rain.

"Let's take a supper break," Josh says around 6:00 p.m. "My parents live nearby." At the house, Josh introduces his parents, Ken and Alice. Alice is in a wheelchair. She uses oxygen to breathe.

Ken is watching hurricane warnings on TV. "We're not leaving," he says. "This is a well-built house. It has withstood hurricanes before. Besides, evacuating would be difficult for Alice."

By the time dinner is over, it's dark outside. "We should get back to the station," you say.

"You go," Josh says. "I have to help my parents."

To help Josh's family, turn to page 57.

To return to the station, turn to page 62.

"I'll stay a while longer," you say. "Take the car. I'll find a ride back to the station. If I stay, I can call in updates. The more information we can provide viewers, the better."

Josh leaves. The entire stretch of beach is now covered with water. It pours over the seawall onto the road.

By 8:00 p.m. you're cold, wet, and windblown. It's time to seek shelter. There's a small convenience store across the street. Its windows are covered with plywood. When you pound on the door, the owner invites you in.

"I'm Nick," he says. "I plan to stay to protect my property."

People board up windows during hurricanes to keep the glass from breaking.

You call Uncle Dave and let him know what's happening. "You have to leave now," he says sternly. "Failure to heed an evacuation order is a crime in Florida."

Turn the page.

When you explain the law to Nick, he says, "But if I leave, looters will break in and steal everything."

Nick's neighbor, Barry, stops by to see if anyone needs a ride to safety. "It's time to go," he says. "There's already several inches of water on the street."

Nick finally agrees. "I'll just pack up a few things and then I'll leave too. My mom lives near the TV station. You can wait and go with me. Or you can go with Barry now."

To go with Barry, turn to page 63.

To wait for Nick, turn to page 64.

You offer to stay to help. "If we can get an ambulance for Alice, we can all leave." But when you try to call 911, you discover that all the telephone circuits are busy.

Josh pulls you aside. "Don't put yourself in danger. I have to stay. You don't. Take the car and go back to the station."

To stay, turn to page **58.**

To Leave, turn to page **62.**

Josh needs you. You help him nail plywood over the windows and glass doors. That will help the house withstand the strong winds. You haul emergency supplies from the basement to the second floor. There are flashlights, extra blankets, and food—crackers, peanut butter, cookies, and some easy-open cans of soup and pasta.

"We have enough food for several days," Josh says. "Now fill the bathtub with water." He hands you several empty bottles. "Fill these too. Extra drinking water is important. And grab my mom's pills if you can."

Josh unplugs all the major appliances and turns off the electricity.

"We're likely to be hit by the storm surge," Ken says. "We should move upstairs now." It takes all three of you to carry Alice to the second floor. You settle her far from the windows. High winds might tear away the plywood and break the glass.

Josh turns on the battery-powered radio in case there's an Emergency Alert System (EAS) message. Despite the roar of the wind, you fall asleep. Around 3:00 a.m. a loud crash wakes you. Wind has torn the shutters off the bedroom window. "At least the roof is holding," Josh says.

The house squeals as if it's being pulled off the foundation. The wind rattles the shutters. Just when you fear that the house will blow away, the wind dies down. Everything is quiet. "Is it over?" Alice asks.

Turn the page.

"Not likely," you say. "I think we're in the eye of the hurricane. Once the eye passes over us, the winds will increase and switch direction."

"Did anyone see Alice's pills?" Ken asks.

"They're on the kitchen table," you say. "I forgot them." You start down the stairs.

"Wait!" Josh says. "The winds could switch direction at any time."

You calculate the odds. The eye could be more than 120 miles in diameter, and since the hurricane might move at only 20 miles per hour, you could be waiting for hours. Of course it could be moving much faster. You'll have to guess.

A hurricane spins around its center, which is called the eye.

*To go downstairs for the pills, turn to page **68**.*

*To wait for the storm to end, turn to page **71**.*

You figure returning to town is the safest choice. But the roads are jammed with people evacuating. The car radio gives updates on the storm. Fred is now a Category 4 and is aiming for a direct hit. Traffic comes to a halt. The radio announcer issues a bulletin: "City officials ask that drivers use recommended routes only." If you follow that advice, it might take hours to reach the station. Maybe you should try a shortcut through the side streets.

To exit to a side street, turn to page **66.**

To stay in traffic, turn to page **67.**

"It's dangerous to wait," you say, accepting Barry's offer. "Nick, you should leave with us."

"I'll leave soon," Nick promises.

Barry guns the car's engine to get through the water flooding the streets. "Hold tight!" he yells as the car goes around a curve. BAM! The car slams into a tree. A big branch lands on top of the car. You push your airbag aside and check on Barry. Blood streams from a cut on his forehead. "I'll be fine," he says as he applies pressure to the cut.

You're about to open the door when you notice several electrical wires draped across the hood. You're in a dangerous situation. Barry needs a doctor, but you don't know if the wires are live.

To stay in the car and wait for help to arrive, turn to page 69.

To leave the car to get help, turn to page 70.

Barry's route will take you miles out of the way, so you decide to wait for Nick. You help him load several boxes of merchandise into his car. By the time you're done, the water is up to the car's hubcaps. When Nick tries to start the car, the engine sputters and dies.

The wind whips palm trees back and forth, rips tiles off the roof, and carries away a small shed. The water is rising.

"We're going to have to go back into the store," Nick shouts above the wind. The building has a small attic above the store. "We'll be safe there," he says. "The water will never rise this high."

The water rises quickly. It doesn't reach the building's top level, but it's so powerful that it carries the store off its foundation and into the swirling waters.

The building collapses, tossing you into the floodwater. You struggle to stay above water, but you're powerless against the waves. You slip beneath the surface, a victim of Hurricane Fred.

THE END

To follow another path, turn to page 11.
To read the conclusion, turn to page 101.

Since traffic is stalled, taking the shortcut seems sensible. You take the nearest exit and begin to speed along neighborhood streets. There's another bridge near Palm Tree Way. You go south on Washington and turn east onto Seaside Terrace. The sky is black, and the winds are howling. The weather is getting worse by the minute. The light turns red as you reach Palm Tree Way. You slam on the brakes, but the car hydroplanes across the rain-slick road.

BOOM! The car stops with a crash, and you die instantly. You never even saw what hit you.

THE END

To follow another path, turn to page 11.
To read the conclusion, turn to page 101.

It's safest to stay on the recommended highway. The exit to the station is only 3 miles away. How long can that take?

With thousands of people evacuating, you inch along for the next two hours before reaching your exit. You travel along neighborhood streets back to the station. These neighborhoods are 3 miles from the coast. Even a strong surge is unlikely to reach this far.

Areas prone to hurricanes often have planned evacuation routes.

HURRICANE EVACUATION ROUTE

Turn to page **73.**

"There's time," you say. The house is quiet. So is the wind. But by the time you reach the first floor, the eye has passed. The storm is traveling much faster than you thought. Hurricane winds batter the house as you fumble around in the darkness. You don't know the layout of the house. You can't find the stairs. As you feel your way along the wall, a huge gust of wind blows the plywood off the picture window. As the window shatters, a shard of glass pierces a major artery in your neck. Blood spurts from the wound. You pass out and fall into the rising water. You'll never know if Josh and his parents survived the storm.

THE END

To follow another path, turn to page 11.
To read the conclusion, turn to page 101.

Getting out of the car is too dangerous. You stay inside and call 911 on your cell phone. You get a busy signal, so you call your uncle at the station. He gets a message to the power company.

The power company employees know exactly how to handle the situation. When they arrive, they shut off the power so that you can escape the car. "That was a close call," one of the workers says. "All downed wires are dangerous. You did the right thing by staying in the car and calling for help." The car is battered, but you can still drive it. You take a recommended route to the station.

Turn to page **73.**

You open the car door and step onto the street. It's the last step you ever take. Inside the car, the rubber tires protected you from the electric current. Outside the car, electricity from the downed wires travels the length of your body. It kills you instantly.

Several people rush to help, but a retired electrician holds them back. "It's too late," he says. "Anyone who gets near those wires risks death." You are a victim of Hurricane Fred.

THE END

To follow another path, turn to page 11.
To read the conclusion, turn to page 101.

It's too dangerous to risk going downstairs. "The medicine can wait," Josh says. "Mom wouldn't want you to take any chances." A few minutes later the winds pick up. This hurricane is moving fast!

The night seems to last forever as the wind howls and the house shakes. By morning the house's first floor is flooded, but the second floor is still dry. You peek out of the window and make a terrible discovery. Most of the neighboring houses are gone. You were lucky to have survived. Thousands of others who refused to leave lost their lives. You'll never challenge a hurricane again.

THE END

To follow another path, turn to page 11.
To read the conclusion, turn to page 101.

The damage caused by hurricanes can take years to clean up.

You sigh with relief as you reach the station's parking lot. You and Uncle Dave spend the night watching Hurricane Fred come ashore. The hurricane takes down trees and electric poles and blows roofs off houses. The storm surge floods many neighborhoods. Luckily most people evacuated in time. They lost their houses and possessions, but not their lives.

THE END

To follow another path, turn to page 11.
To read the conclusion, turn to page 101.

Floodwaters can be strong enough to wash away vehicles.

CHAPTER 4

Flood!

The only summer job you can find is at your dad's hardware store. "Make the best of it," your professor says. "If your county offers CERT classes, sign up." CERT stands for Community Emergency Response Team. The training will teach you how to prepare for disasters and help during emergencies.

Your classes start July 1. Scott Brown, your instructor, explains that in a major disaster there won't be enough emergency responders. CERT training prepares citizens to care for themselves, their families, and the community. CERT volunteers have helped in fires, floods, and storms.

Your classmates include men and women of all ages. Some are college students, two are nurses, and one is a Boy Scout leader.

"It's important to know what disasters are likely to strike this community," Scott says. "For instance, we're not likely to experience a hurricane." Everyone laughs. You live 1,000 miles from the ocean. "But flash floods are a possible problem here after all this spring rain."

Flash floods kill about 200 people a year in the United States. More than half of all flood deaths happen in cars. A car begins to float in 2 feet of water. Fast-moving water can carry a car or truck off a bridge into the river. The road itself may crumble and fall into the river, and underpasses quickly fill with water. "The county has a water rescue unit trained to deal with water rescues," Scott explains. "We volunteers never enter the water to try to save someone."

As you drive home that night, you're thinking about the July 4th holiday. Your parents have already left town to visit friends. Your brother, Dan, is going camping. What will you do?

You wake up on July 4 to the familiar sound of rain pounding on the roof. When you turn on the radio, a weather bulletin interrupts the music:

"The National Weather Service has issued a flash flood warning. Runoff from excessive rainfall is causing flash flooding. Do not attempt to travel across flooded roads. Find alternate routes. It only takes a few inches of swiftly flowing water to carry vehicles away."

The phone rings. It's Aunt Jean. She lives in Big River Mobile Home Park, on the banks of Big River. "I'm getting nervous," she says. "The river is rising. The police say I may have to evacuate. But I can't find my cat, Ruby. Will you help me?"

Turn the page.

You hesitate. You're worried about your brother, Dan. He's camping at Hazard State Park near Big River Dam. If there's a flood, Dan could also be in danger.

To help Aunt Jean, turn to page **79**.

To warn Dan at the campground, turn to page **81**.

Aunt Jean is almost 80. She'll need your help to evacuate. You try to call Dan, but you can't get through. He's probably on his way home. He knows enough to move to higher ground whenever a river or stream becomes muddy. Streams that are only 6 inches deep can swell to 10 feet during a downpour.

It rained all night, and the rain isn't letting up. "Four inches have fallen in the last hour," the radio announcer says. "Stay off the roads if at all possible."

Flash floods can occur with little warning.

Turn the page.

You can't stay off the roads if you're going to help Aunt Jean. River Street is the shortest route to the mobile home park. There's a low spot at the intersection of Main and River streets. Cars splash through the water up to their hubcaps. Maybe you should take Hall Street. The elevation on Hall Street is higher. But taking that route will delay you at least 15 minutes.

To go through the water, turn to page 82.

To turn around to take Hall Street, turn to page 83.

The emergency radio is sitting on the shelf in the kitchen. Dan forgot to take it. You try to call him, but he doesn't answer his cell. Cell phones don't work well in remote areas. You had better drive to Hazard State Park, hike to the campsite, and warn Dan about the flood.

The car radio gives the latest weather bulletins. "The police have just issued evacuation orders for Big River Mobile Home Park." Good. The police will help Aunt Jean leave. You focus on the rainy roads. When you reach River Street, you notice cars splashing through the water. You can't even see the surface of the road. River Street is the shortest route to the state park. Taking another route is sure to slow you down.

*To go through the water, turn to page **82**.*

*To turn around to take another route, turn to page **85**.*

You drive through the flooded street. Water sprays up onto your windshield. Suddenly the car plunges into a water-filled pothole. When you push down on the accelerator, the car hydroplanes across the slick road. You slam on the gas pedal and twist the wheel, but nothing happens. You're sliding toward the riverbank. The car slips down the steep bank and plunges into the fast-moving river. You have only seconds to act.

To turn off the engine and unfasten your seat belt, turn to page **96**.

To leave the car running and open the window, turn to page **97**.

You turn around and take Hall Street. It's never safe to drive through flooded streets. It's not safe to walk either. Six inches of fast-moving water is enough to knock you off your feet. The rain doesn't let up as you drive into the mobile home park. Water is rising up the sides of the mobile homes. A police officer stops you at the entrance. "We have orders to evacuate the park," he says.

Water on a flooded street can be deeper than you think it is.

Turn the page.

"I'm here to pick up my aunt," you tell him.

"Good. We don't have much time. We're worried about a crack in Big River Dam. If the dam bursts, this entire park will be underwater."

There's no time to waste. You drive to Violet Lane and pull into Aunt Jean's driveway. She greets you at the door. "Ruby's still missing! I can't leave without her."

Just then you hear a meow. "She's on the roof," Aunt Jean says. "There's a ladder attached to the side of the house."

To leave immediately, turn to page 93.

To climb onto the roof after the cat, turn to page 94.

It's never safe to try to drive through standing water. You have no idea how deep it might be. You don't even know the condition of the road beneath the water. Fast-moving water can make pavement crumble.

You turn around and take a different route. Rain hammers the roof of the car. The windshield wipers struggle to keep the windows clear. You reach the park and pull into the big parking lot that overlooks the river. The parking lot is high and dry. There's a service road that winds along at the river's edge, but it's too dangerous to drive beside the river.

Turn the page.

You get out and begin running toward the campground. By the time you get there, you're wet and chilled. A boy is standing at the water's edge. "Dan!" you call as you run toward him. But it's not Dan. This boy is much younger. He's crying. "I'm Brandon," he says. "My friend Alan fell in the river. He's drowning!"

Alan is about 10 feet from shore, struggling to stay afloat. "Help!" he screams. His eyes are wide with fear.

To go for help, go to page **87**.

To jump in after him, turn to page **92**.

You need to get help, but your cell phone isn't working. You tell Brandon to run to the ranger station. You feel calmer now. Going for help was an important first step. "We're getting help!" you shout to Alan. You want to keep him calm. If he panics, he'll be in even more danger.

You may be able to pull yourself out of floodwater by grabbing a tree branch.

Turn the page.

You take a moment to study the situation. Alan is holding on to a tree branch. Normally the tree would be on dry land, but the river is rising. "Hold on, Alan!" you yell. "Don't let go."

You try to reach out, but Alan's too far from shore. What other choices do you have? There's a canoe tied to a nearby tree. A long rope dangles from the tree to the canoe. You untie the rope. There are two paddles inside the canoe.

To consider other options, go to page 89.

To paddle out to get the boy, turn to page 99.

Trained rescuers can use a boat for rescues, but you're not a trained rescuer. It's not safe for you to take a canoe into the flooded river. You'll have to find another way. Maybe you can use the paddle. You hold onto a sturdy tree and extend the paddle. "Grab it, Alan!"

Alan desperately grabs for the paddle, but he can't reach it. You toss the paddle aside. There's a long rope coiled inside the canoe. You fling the rope into the water. It lands just short of the boy. You try again. He grabs it on the third try. "Now hold tight, and I'll pull you to shore," you tell him.

Turn the page.

It takes all your strength to drag Alan to shore. He's freezing. You toss your jacket over him. "Let's get back to the ranger station. You can warm up there." You look around for Dan, but there's no sign of him or his friends. You hope that he's somewhere safe.

The ranger meets you on the trail. Brandon is with him. "I heard you needed help," the ranger says. Then he asks how you rescued Alan. "Good choice," he says. "It's very dangerous to swim or boat in floodwaters."

It's a relief to get home. Dan is already there. He says he and his friends left the campground as soon as the river started rising. "We left our tent and all of our gear at the campsite."

Authorities, such as park rangers, can help in times of emergency.

"That's OK," you tell him. "Things can be replaced, but you can't."

THE END

To follow another path, turn to page 11.
To read the conclusion, turn to page 101.

You jump into the swirling waters. "Hold on! I'm coming," you yell to the boy.

The water quickly overpowers you and carries you downstream. You're a strong swimmer, but you can't fight the current. The water begins pulling you under. You hold your breath as long as you can. You gasp for air, but gulp water instead. In a matter of seconds, you lose consciousness. Your last thought is of Alan, the boy you were trying to rescue. You hope that someone else was able to save him.

THE END

To follow another path, turn to page 11.
To read the conclusion, turn to page 101.

"I'm sorry, Aunt Jean, but we have to leave. The water is rising. Besides, it's not safe to climb onto that metal roof in the rain. It's just too slippery."

"What about Ruby?" Aunt Jean cries.

Then you remember something you heard in CERT class. "Once we get to safety we'll call Animal Rescue. There are organizations that send volunteers to disaster areas to rescue pets. They'll come for Ruby."

You help Aunt Jean to the car and quickly drive to your house. You're relieved to find Dan there. Your decision saved Aunt Jean's life. Ruby survived too, thanks to the animal rescue group.

THE END

To follow another path, turn to page 11.
To read the conclusion, turn to page 101.

Aunt Jean loves her cat. You slosh through the rising water to the ladder and climb to the roof. Ruby is sitting on the far edge. "Here, kitty," you call again and again.

But Ruby doesn't move. She stares at you and hisses. You creep closer on your hands and knees. The metal roof is slick. Maybe you can grab the cat's collar. But when you reach out, she darts away. You lunge after her and feel yourself sliding off the roof. "Help!" you call, but there's no one to rescue you. Aunt Jean is inside packing Ruby's food.

You fling your arms out, but there's nothing to grab. You fall headfirst into the water that surrounds Aunt Jean's home. You're alive, but unconscious from hitting your head on the ground. No one saw you slide off the roof, so no one can rescue you. You drown with your face in only 4 inches of water.

Animal rescuers are trained to save pets during natural disasters.

THE END

To follow another path, turn to page 11.
To read the conclusion, turn to page 101.

You turn off the engine and undo your seat belt. As the car hits the murky water, you struggle to open the door. But the water pressure makes that impossible. Your heart is pounding. You gulp for air and swallow water. The car flips and sinks below the river's surface. Without a seat belt to hold you in place, you slip and slide inside the sinking car.

Water is filling the car. You try to find the window. If you can open it, you can slip out. But you can't find the window. You can't see anything in the murky water. Divers discover the car a few days later. Your lifeless body is trapped inside.

THE END

To follow another path, turn to page 11.
To read the conclusion, turn to page 101.

The car sinks beneath the surface. You take a deep breath and try to stay calm. You leave the engine running, keep your seat belt on, and open the window as fast as you can. That will help the car flood quickly. As the car flips over, you grab the window frame. That open window is your escape route. Holding on to it can mean the difference between life and death.

Even though you know what to do, your heart begins pounding as water fills the car. You've never been so scared in your life. You take a last gulp of air and hold your breath as water covers your neck and head. It takes only seconds for the car to fill with water. Then you release your seat belt and slip out the open window. You push your body upward until your head pops above the water's surface. You grab a sturdy tree branch and use it to pull yourself onto the riverbank.

Turn the page.

You nearly lost your life. Your training saved you this time, but you'll never drive on flooded roads again.

HOW TO
Escape From a Submerged Car:

1. Don't panic. Stay calm.

2. Keep your seat belt on.

3. The second your car hits the water, open the window.

4. Grab the window frame and hold on.

5. As soon as the car floods, undo your seat belt and swim out of the vehicle.

6. Don't go back into the vehicle

THE END

To follow another path, turn to page 11.
To read the conclusion, turn to page 101.

You push the canoe into the water and hop in. Before you can even dip the paddles into the water, the river takes over. It carries the canoe downstream, away from Alan.

You struggle to turn around, but the river is in control. You grab the seat with both hands as the canoe races through the water. Tree limbs and an old refrigerator float nearby. You're caught in the current. The canoe is heading for the concrete supports of Big River Bridge. You shift your weight, trying to change the canoe's direction. But the current is too strong. The canoe slams into the bridge. You fly through the air and hit your head on the refrigerator. The blow kills you before the water can.

THE END

To follow another path, turn to page 11.
To read the conclusion, turn to page 101.

Dangerous storms
can develop quickly.

CHAPTER 5

Survival Guide

Chances are you'll never face a weather emergency. But if you do, knowing what to do could mean the difference between life and death. The first step to survival is being prepared. You should know what kinds of storms are likely to occur in your area and what to do when the National Weather Service issues a storm warning. Be sure everyone in your family knows how to call 911. Are there other numbers you should know, such as your parents' work numbers or grandmother's home number? If so, make a list and memorize it.

Help your family develop an emergency plan. If you live along the coast, how will you deal with hurricanes? Do you have an evacuation plan? Where will you go if you are ordered to leave? If tornadoes are likely in your area, decide ahead of time where you'll wait out the storm. The basement is always the best choice. If you don't have a basement, choose a bathroom or other interior room and stay away from windows. If you live in a mobile home, you must find another shelter. Be sure to have a designated meeting place in case your family is separated during an emergency.

An emergency shelter is designed to withstand strong storms.

Prepare an emergency kit. Include flashlights, a battery-operated radio or TV, and extra batteries. You'll also need water and food. You should store at least one gallon of water per person per day and change the water every six months. Choose foods that don't require cooking or added water. Buy or make a basic first aid kit. If possible, take a first aid class through school, a Scout troop, or the Red Cross.

Storm emergencies are never fun. But taking the time to prepare for them and learning what to do if they happen makes them a little less frightening.

Prepare an emergency kit before you need it.

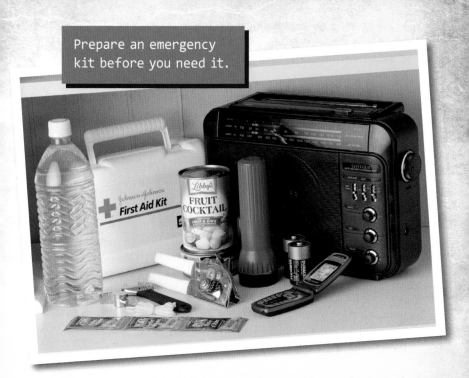

REAL SURVIVORS

Reed Timmer, *tornado chaser*

Extreme meteorologist Reed Timmer has seen dozens of tornadoes. Timmer, whose adventures are featured on the Discovery Channel's *Storm Chasers*, has always been fascinated by the weather. He and his crew not only film dramatic storm footage, they also let people ride along in their storm-chasing vehicle, The Dominator. The Dominator is protected by 8,000 pounds of armor and bulletproof windows. It has survived 200-mph tornado winds. Timmer hopes his research will make it possible to warn people sooner of upcoming storms.

Stephanie Abrams, *hurricane reporter*

Stephanie Abrams is a meteorologist and co-host of the Weather Channel's *Wake Up With Al* and *Your Weather Today*. If a hurricane is predicted, she and other reporters go to the scene days ahead of time. They check the area, set up equipment, and store supplies such as food and water in case they are stranded by the storm. In 2010 Abrams traveled to North Carolina to cover Hurricane Earl. Her most memorable storm was 2005's Hurricane Katrina.

Raquel Dawson, *flash flood survivor*
Seventeen-year-old Raquel Dawson of Oklahoma City, Oklahoma, was going to work June 14, 2010, when she noticed a woman stranded in her car on a flooded street. Dawson waded through deep water and helped the woman get to a line of trees. Then Dawson began swimming for help. She tried to make it to the road. But the current got stronger, and she made little progress. A television helicopter pilot spotted Dawson. Rescuers sent an airboat to the rescue. The airboat capsized, but two other boats were able to rescue Dawson and those in the first rescue boat.

Morgan Hayden and Joe Moton, *tornado survivors*
When a tornado ripped through Yazoo City, Mississippi, April 25, 2010, Morgan Hayden and her boyfriend, Joe Moton, rushed into the bathroom. They huddled in the bathtub. The tornado destroyed the entire house—except for the bathroom. Neither Hayden nor Moton was injured, but 10 others in rural Mississippi died that day.

Christine McLaren, *flash flood survivor*
In December 2010 Christine McLaren tried to cross a flooded road near her home in Redridge, Australia. A wall of water slammed into her car and washed her into deep water. McLaren remained calm. She opened a window and crawled onto the roof of the car. The water kept rising, but two men in a small boat pulled her to safety.

SURVIVAL QUIZ

1. What's the first thing you should do if your car becomes submerged in water?

A. Turn off the car.

B. Unbuckle your seat belt.

C. Roll down the window.

2. If you are traveling in a car when a tornado strikes what should you do?

A. Stop the car under a tree or underpass.

B. Get out of the car and crouch low to the ground.

C. Try to outdrive the tornado.

3. What is the safest place during a hurricane?

A. No place is safe. Evacuate the area at once using a recommended route.

B. The top story of a large office building.

C. A basement.

Answers: C, B, A.

READ MORE

Doeden, Matt. *How to Survive a Flood.* Mankato, Minn.: Capstone Press, 2009.

Fradin, Judith Bloom, and Dennis B. Fradin. *Hurricanes.* Washington, D.C.: National Geographic, 2007.

Prokos, Anna. *Tornadoes.* Pleasantville, N.Y.: Gareth Stevens Pub., 2009.

Raum, Elizabeth. *Surviving Hurricanes.* Chicago: Raintree, 2012.

INTERNET SITES

Use FactHound to find Internet sites related to this book. All of the sites on FactHound have been researched by our staff.

Here's all you do:
Visit *www.facthound.com*
Type in this code: 9781429665872

GLOSSARY

catastrophic (kat-uh-STROF-ik)—extremely damaging

debris (duh-BREE)—the scattered pieces of something that has been broken or destroyed

devastating (DEV-uh-stay-ting)—badly damaging or destructive

evacuation (i-va-kyuh-WAY-shun)—the removal of large numbers of people from an area during a time of danger

funnel cloud (FUHN-uhl KLOUD)—a cone-shaped cloud that is usually a visible part of a tornado; a funnel cloud is wide at the top and narrow at the bottom

hydroplane (HYE-druh-playn)—to skim over the surface of water

mandatory (MAN-duh-tor-ee)—required by law

meteorologist (mee-tee-ur-AWL-uh-jist)—a person who studies and predicts the weather

paramedic (pa-ruh-MEH-dik)—a person who treats sick and injured people

radar (RAY-dar)—a weather tool that sends out microwaves to determine the size, strength, and movement of storms

storm surge (STORM SURJ)—a sudden, strong rush of water that happens as a hurricane moves onto land

supercell (SOO-pur-sel)—a large, rotating thunderstorm

BIBLIOGRAPHY

Bechtel, Stefan, and Tim Samaras. *Tornado Hunter: Getting Inside the Most Violent Storms on Earth.* Washington, D.C.: National Geographic, 2009.

Bluestein, Howard B. *Tornado Alley: Monster Storms of the Great Plains.* New York: Oxford University Press, 1999.

Burt, Christopher C. *Extreme Weather: A Guide and Record Book.* New York: W. W. Norton, 2007.

Emanuel, Kerry. *Divine Wind: The History and Science of Hurricanes.* New York: Oxford University Press, 2005.

Fitzpatrick, Patrick J. *Natural Disasters, Hurricanes: A Reference Handbook.* Santa Barbara, Calif.: ABC-CLIO, 1999.

Gibson, Christine. *Extreme Natural Disasters.* New York: Collins, 2007.

Sheets, Bob, and Jack Williams. *Hurricane Watch: Forecasting the Deadliest Storms on Earth.* New York: Vintage, 2001.

Svenvold, Mark. *Big Weather: Chasing Tornadoes in the Heart of America.* New York: Henry Holt, 2005.

INDEX

Abrams, Stephanie, 106

Community Emergency Response Team (CERT), 75, 93

Dawson, Raquel, 107

Emergency Alert System (EAS), 59
emergency kits, 27, 58, 104
emergency numbers, 101
emergency plans, 102

flooding
    animal rescues, 93, 94
    boat rescues, 89, 99, 107
    cars, 76, 77, 80, 81, 82, 83, 85, 96, 97, 98, 107
    damage, 9, 76
    deaths, 9, 76
    evacuations, 78, 79–80, 81, 83–84
    warnings, 77

Hayden, Morgan, 107
hurricanes
    categories, 44, 45, 50, 62
    damage, 10, 59, 64–65, 68, 71, 73
    direction, 45, 53, 60
    electricity, 63, 66, 69, 70
    emergency supplies, 52, 58, 106
    evacuations, 46, 51, 52, 53, 54, 55, 56, 62, 67, 73, 102
    eye, 60, 68
    formation, 10
    rainfall, 49, 53, 66
    seasons, 44
    shelter, 54, 58, 64
    sizes, 10, 60
    speeds, 60, 71
    storm surges, 10, 49, 51, 59, 67, 73
    Track Forecast Cones, 45

tracking equipment, 44
warnings, 45, 46, 49, 53
winds, 10, 44, 45, 46, 47, 49, 51, 58, 59, 60, 64, 66, 68, 71

McLaren, Christine, 107
meteorologists, 7, 8, 43, 106
Moton, Joe, 107

National Hurricane Center, 44, 45, 50
National Weather Service, 16, 21, 39, 40, 77, 101

Saffir-Simpson Hurricane Wind Scale, 44, 45
Skywarn, 40

Timmer, Reed, 106
tornadoes
    damage, 8, 23, 24, 27, 32, 34, 35, 36, 37, 38
    deaths, 22, 107
    debris, 23, 25, 27, 38, 39, 40
    formation, 8, 15, 16, 17–18, 21
    funnel clouds, 16, 18, 19, 22, 23, 25–26, 28, 34, 35, 36, 37, 41
    hailstones, 15, 28, 29
    rainfall, 20, 25, 28
    ratings, 39
    shelter, 24, 30, 34, 35, 36, 37, 38, 41, 102, 107
    speeds, 19, 24, 39, 106
    supercell thunderstorms, 8, 16, 21
    Tornado Alley, 8, 9
    tracking equipment, 14
    wall clouds, 17–18
    warnings, 8, 22, 25, 40, 41
    winds, 15, 23, 24, 25, 31, 36, 37, 38, 39, 106